Unhurried Vision

Books by Michael Rothenberg

What The Fish Saw
(Twowindows Press, 1984)

Nightmare Of The Violins
(Twowindows Press, 1986),

Man/Woman
(Big Bridge Press, 1988)

Favorite Songs
(Big Bridge Press, 1990)

Punk Rockwell
(Tropical Press, 2000)

The Paris Journals
(Fish Drum, 2000)

Grown Up Cuba
(Il Begatto Press, 2003)

Editor:
Overtime: Selected Poems —Philip Whalen
(Viking Penguin, 1999)

As Ever: Selected Poems—Joanne Kyger
(Penguin Books, 2002)

Unhurried Vision

Michael Rothenberg

La Alameda Press :: Albuquerque

THE FOLLOWING POEMS HAVE APPEARED IN THESE PUBLICATIONS:
"Legend", 5_Trope; "Unhurried Vision", CrossConnect; "Small Things In Life",
Disquieting Muses; "Scientific Fact", Exquisite Corpse; "Heart Sutra", Fish Drum;
"Celebration", "August 22, 1999", "Ocean Restaurant", "On Time", "4th Floor",
"Sustenance", Fulcrum; "Ongoing", Jacket; "Pilgrims", Mike & Dale's Younger Poets;
"My Whole Body Shakes With Creation", milk; "Consuming Passions",
"Even The Bad Die Young", Moveo Angelus; "Over Time", "War Poem",
Poems for Peace; "Airport Telephone Interzone", Prosodia; "Howard",
"Sustenance", RealPoetik; "Impulses & Obsessions", The 3rd Page;
"Choose", Transit; and "October 20, 1999", Unlikely Stories

Special thanks to Joanne Kyger, Rofiah Breen and Terri Carrion

Cover painting: Richard Diebenkorn, (1922-1993)
Interior with a Book, 1959
oil on canvas; 70 x 64 inches (1787.8 x 162.6 cm.)
THE NELSON-ATKINS MUSEUM OF ART, KANSAS CITY, MISSOURI
(GIFT OF THE FRIENDS OF ART) F63-15   PHOTO CREDIT: E.G. SCHEMPF

Frontispiece: "The End of the line / Nasturtiums"—ink on paper
Endpiece: "The end, of a month of Sundays"—ink on paper
from Highgrade: Doodles, Poems by Philip Whalen (Coyote's Journal, 1966)
Permission of the Literary Estate of Philip Whalen

Photograph of the author by Terri Carrion

Library of Congress Cataloging-in-Publication Data

Rothenberg, Michael.
Unhurried vision : poems / Michael Rothenberg.
p. cm.
ISBN 1-888809-40-X (alk. paper)
I. Title.

PS3568.O8619U54 2003
811'.54--dc22

2003018385

La Alameda Press
9636 Guadalupe Trail NW
Albuquerque, New Mexico 87114

I dedicate this year to you, Philip Whalen

The End of the line.

    Carefully try to remember what
    it is that you are doing. "How
    do you do? How do you like
    what you do?" are you going
    to continue in the same wasteful
    and thoughtless fashion ?

21 v 64
Philip Whalen

Nasturtiums
22 V 64

Longing

Something gone again
— my paper horn alone until midnight

    Sirens scream in unison

The table-saw in the garage rings out
a dusty-throated machine-head complaint
against wood

The picket fence is electrified

       Hedge, motion-sensored
       cameras positioned to detect

a breath, light
flash
or when the raccoon scuttles—
a crime

an instance of creative success
The long call of desire

       imbedded in my head

January 31, 1999: LEGEND

Talk to me in any language
I'll stop talking
Make meaning clearer

More naked and I become more
practiced in my dance
along the nerve

It's raining
now everywhere around
dousing all the flames at sea

February 17: ELEPHANTS

Olson was a great talker

Ponderous Gloucester
Poundian absurdiana

Mountains of speed, pills, alcohol
When his liver gave out

       Whalen said
       he found himself

       crying big tears
       unaccountably

       then finished his pork noodles

*

They could trace
the appearance of asterisks

with the concurrence
       of elephants bathing

*

That duck wears a hat in the rain
Navy surplus poncho. Cane

pokes down the worn granite
        Steps off the curb

March 22: CHOOSE

I have a clue
Monkeys like to be left alone

They don't smoke cigars or play poker
Prefer not to dress up like The Three Bears
But a man's got to do what a man's got to do

Sunflower seeds, bananas, peanuts
Making industry out of ecology
10,000 years of giving up
Now we're supposed to compromise

So we take what's left and split it
Take what's left and split
Until everything is in ownership

And no one can live
Because there are too many fences
Up to the moon and across the cosmos

March 24: IKEBANA

That was good

A prairie sunflower

    Blown back
    By a semi

        On a Montana
        Highway

A community of
Roses

Gathered
For an occasion

        Florida!

    Add greens & a spray
Of baby's-breath

        When you walk in
        It's you

You're walking into

What goes around comes
Around

Invention
To send

Sorrow south

Your bunch of
Beauties

      Smelling
      Up the bouquet

When the work is done

March 25: CELEBRATION

When he smiled
there was a hole in his head
And though blind
his eyes flung open wide
as two moons on a pink plate

Bald and pink and great
This is a man you could love
And the poetry he makes
can jump out the window
and get away fast

    But here he is
    Margarita on the rocks
    Glass of cabernet sauvignon
    Bowl of pasta, the curly kind in feta and marinara
    A hot French roll

    And I'm talking about the lessons
    The great teachers and *Patterson* and Crane and Forrest Read
    Inventing the wheel again

        "My problem is I don't drink enough"

There's more to the sky than meets the eye

"My secret agenda is
    I want the reader to stumble on things
    they don't know and want to find more about"

You mean you want them to read more?
I wipe my plate clean

        "Yes"

April 3: EVEN THE BAD DIE YOUNG

How can someone full of intellect be so empty headed?

April 6: OVER TIME

Even when that bamboo bends
            it can support a sitting man
                        drinking green tea

            Way back before he learned
            to count the fingers on his hand

            he collected rocks and
            brought them to his garden
            of snails and slugs

                        Head on a pillow
                        Under four blankets
                        Socks on and squinting

At the theater in my head
We've become good friends

April 8: UNHURRIED VISION

Purple berries
Maybe they are grapes
I don't know from where

I feel some trembling
In my stomach and spine
I shake my feet to shake it off

Build up a hunger so the berries
Will be sweeter than nature
A hallucination of desire

Juice soaked flesh
Breaking under pressure
Of tongue and blind caress

Nectar of honeysuckle
Waves rolling sugar rich
Hanging there in sweat

April 11: CONSUMING PASSIONS

Put your slippers on
Come up here
I need to talk to you

I know it's night and raining
And the hall is filthy
And you've only got those
puffy white slippers
to keep your feet warm
but I've got something
important to say

Hurry!
You can always
wash your slippers but this
situation, well, who knows
It may never occur again

                                *

                    You didn't like it
                    For some reason
                    It had too much
                    Personality
                    Is a fine thing
                    So far away

And only you can measure
The degree of your ignorance
Personality is not your father

April 12: 4 & 20 BLACKBIRDS

When I take Valium
I don't care

Wake in the night
Don't know which side
of the bed to get off

Where's the middle of the night?
Which bed and room?
Stumbling in a nod

It's a risk being
comfortably confused
But it sure beats the panic

April 14: WAR POEM

Move in closer
Your dreams are for sale

The green curry chicken
Halibut in garlic sauce will save the day

Bring a blanket
Sit down on the beach in the rain
Watch the waves

Someone loves you and

Someday if you need babies
To add to your Victory Parade
You can have some

April 20: THE PAST IN REFLECTION OF THE FUTURE

Coming down out of control
Peregrine, sea lion
Guardians of the garden

      My "master" is my friend
      We go eat green curry chicken
      Drink margaritas
      Then he tells me he owes me one

      Famed for his ill-temper
      He's gentle
      and sings corny songs
      from radio 70 years ago

      And when he goes I will be alone
      Then who will sit with me
      Console me
      in the shade of poetry?

The street goes down to the corner
Across the street
Up the street to the corner
Cross the street to the other side
Then once more there's a corner

We cross and crisscrossing
We are back at the table
Slurping noodles
to fill our bellies with peace

Any day now I will go and celebrate
my master among strangers

April 28: IS STORMY WEATHER YOUR FAVORITE SONG?

(Stormy Weather?) "not really"
_____

Falling In Love
  "from Blue Angel by Marlene Dietrich"
_____

Footsteps On The Ceilings
_____

Night & Day
_____

Who Cares? (Gershwin)
_____

Our Love Is Here To Stay
_____

  "songs from Victor Herbert & Sigmund Romberg"
_____

Pale Hands
  "1890's"
_____

I'm Only A Bird In A Golden Cage
_____

  "all these things I'm likely to sing in the bathtub"
_____

Beyond The Blue Horizon

Mighty Like A Rose

> "If you ever saw Mr. Robert Montgomery carrying a
> head around in hatbox, also a favorite of Harpo Marx
> because of its complicated cadenza which he could
> stretch out endlessly"

(Any other requests?)

> "songs from Porgy & Bess"

Summertime, It Ain't Necessarily So

Top Hat

Only A Rose

> "that one my parents used to like"

My Hero, Come Hero Mine

> "and Joanne Kyger sang:
>> 'Thou Art Divine
>> The True Doo Doo Fantasy of Heaven'"

April 29: PASSIVE OBSESSION

Sorry, I can't make it tonight I've got a life too

      But you don't care
      And I can't sleep late

I've got nowhere to go

          Turn up the volume
          Turn down the voice

It isn't so beautiful
No matter what you think

          So I'm gonna leave town
          Go do my job
          Where I won't be recognized
          Don't have to answer to anyone

      I can get cocky
      But confidence is good
      Ask for what you want

A private dinner with a close friend
Prepared by a gourmet chef

          So nice of you to ask

It's all flattery
But is it love or submission?

    Working both ends against the middle
    It would be nice to get things right

        without a margin of error

I don't need references

        Lamp in a movie
        Shower in a movie
        Cops and robbers chase and escape

It's possible to be familiar
But it's not good enough

    So call when you get in
    I'm gonna be busy

        Learning to operate the equipment
        That can make you or break you

Come on step up to bat
Take your best shot

    How else do you expect to repair
    this seamless existence?

April 30: SMALL THINGS IN LIFE

Close my hand around a moth
Carry it outside

By then the wings are powder

And the baffled aviator does
A nose dive into the brick-paved altar

A tragedy we're here to eulogize

Sometimes it helps to remember
where we are and why
we are where we are and so

I read from NY Today
online calendar — *New York Times,*
Tuesday, May 4, 1999

Buddhist abbot, language poet, Beat affiliate feted in absentia by
peers, devotees. Aging Whalen once roomed with poets Gary Snyder
and Lew Welch (who vanished mysteriously in 1971), resides in San
Francisco "by turns cranky, amused, hungry or sated with experi-
ence" for the latter half of this century. Tributants include: grand
poobah Language poetry Charles Bernstein, Poet/critic Leslie
Scalapino, who wrote introduction to *Overtime* recently published
collected (should say selected) works (PENGUIN). Editor, Michael
Rothenberg will participate with assortment of veterans from New
York's postmodern poetry trenches (Eileen Myles, Ron Padgett,
Jackson MacLow among them). Poetry Project staffers Anselm
Berrigan and Wanda Phipps will take part in this celebration of a
poet whose credo — "I shall be myself" — does not belie his en-
ergy or accomplishments. Admission $7. May 5, 1999.

May 24: *SOMETHING I STOLE FROM A FRIEND*

1 OMEN

Every other day there are dead people
in my dream. They are trying to feed me
The only difference is the menu

2 MENU

Potato soup with sour cream on it
It was delicious
And I wanted more
But there was no more

June 3: MY WHOLE BODY SHAKES WITH CREATION

My whole body shakes with creation
Hive, herd, migration
from cold feet to groin
Hanging around
there for a while, moves on
Quakes where hunger pretends a craving
Catches me with sharp claws
at the lung's root and forces a sigh, escapes

I feel better then
It begins again as if
I had something on my mind
Worrying about something
Love could be enough for a while

Nature wants to escape from the idea
Plum blossoms from a concept
Turtle eggs hatch a great arrival on a beach in a novel

It's a small room
I want to put shells, blue china
a book of Joanne Kyger's, a slab of paradise
pain from the bodies of loved ones
broken lung and burning bone
in a hermetically sealed box
far from the hands of mischief

curiosity or a bum rap
wherever I can find the space

And when I'm surrounded and understand
the treasures I have gathered
I hope to hear music
It keeps my body still, it calms me
Music calms me

June 18: PALE PORTRAIT

Some spell of ink & fire
spent upon the age

Lime pit for the corpse of an experiment

Umbrella blown into the limbs
Branches thatched over never-ending hour

Here I am again talking with angels

June 19: STANDUP ROUTINE

My friends have come to expect a kind of humor
stand up gag or admission of foolishness
to make the way

          a little lighter

                  *

I've lost my sense of humor
      I may find it any place any minute now

        "Don't despair, the earth will survive
            maybe like the moon
                but it will make it
        outlive the libraries, human voice, a rock
        will, has, since before France
        or a footprint in a place now named France
        or many reasons"

More of which concerns me ten seconds later

                  *

When my memory was not so good
and stories that made sense
failed to sustain themselves in my eye

I began remembering children's jokes
brought home from my son's 2nd grade class
That worked for awhile
until he stopped writing my material

*

HA!

June 20-23: NAROPA, SUMMER, THE BEAT LEGACY

1 NIGHT BEFORE GOING

Invitations hard to come by
like some genera of high altitude
        bromeliaceae offered

I go to be in the company of green
        petals and bearded leaves

At night the fragrance stronger

2 GOING AFTER

To speak of legacy is to almost do autobiography. So before I go off the deep end introducing you to my ambiguity, let me say that the "Beat Legacy" is enormous, great, diverse, and stop here for now.

I don't usually write out what I'm going to say. In most forums, writers of critique or gossiping historians are bound by exposition, but my faculty for exposition seems to be malfunctioning.

Still, enthusiasm is at play, and I don't want to miss this opportunity to answer the questions I assume my presence requires. So, if I've left something out, or if there's something you'd like clarified or elaborated, ask me anything, but how much Philip Whalen received from his GI Bill for tuition at Reed College.

Anne Waldman shouts from the audience, "How much?"

June 21, 1999

3 GOING ON

Econo–Lodge, Arapahoe

Ginsberg gone
McClure sleeping down the hall
Philip in jacket blurbs, bio
       summaries & poems
              pieced together

I could be talking about strangers
This could be my family
Dead, sleeping, blind

4 On & On

Showered and shaved
Waiting for cologne to dissipate
before sitting in on a workshop

Patio by parking lot
Two redheads want me to take
their picture for old time's sake
I never knew them

Sipping coffee
Quick thought of The Academy
Worried about the abundance of gerunds
The responsibilities of a poet
Antique or avant garde?

I want a cologne that smells like a whole earth
vegetarian restaurant:

> 9 grain, hummus, curry, mint, dash
> splash on the raw spots, garlic & onion
> lecithin, soothe the chafe

I'm a dead give-away

Scribbling in a note pad
Stinking of French cologne

Fugitive baby
boomer yuppie schlepping
stigma through a meadow
of day-glow flowers

June 22, 1999

5 "ON BEAR'S HEAD"

I dedicate this year to you, Philip Whalen
       falling down the stairs

                 June 23, 1 a.m.

6 Ontological

Pacing back and forth in the motel room
headache from high altitude and air-conditioning
wondering where I'm going to next

Stockbroker calls from Florida to sell me mutual funds
Tells me how the next ten years are gonna be great for growth
"Have you got any 'green' funds, I might be interested in that"

I need more coffee
so I go down to the lobby and get more coffee

He wants to sell me on a "bull market"
Those guys are crazy, "blah, blah, blah internet, buzz, blah"
I think about product like losing contact with myself

"You sound just like one of them"
 I am one of them
And likely to become *more* one of them by and by
One of them professors or knows-about-something people
Seminarians under Big Top at Naropa

Summer heat

I'm going to start weighing out my product
See if there's measurable change. If there's cumulative increase
More or less rare bears?

"Well hell, let's go out into the woods and weigh their poop and find out. That's a good idea"

That's a *real* good idea!

June 23, 1999

7 On Time

On the possibility of revolution
On civil disobedience
On social responsibility
On falling down and getting up
On consciousness and monastic isolation
On plums & pears, agate & jasper, hash & honey, love & money
On Marlene Dietrich & Dharma
On wild sorrow and war
On "Literary Life in the Golden West"

> "I'll tell you about fucking life in the golden west, literary
> life in the golden west. While we're downstairs sitting
> zazen someone got in here stole everyone's wallets out
> of their jackets. There's no literary life in the golden
> west. That's fucking literary life in the golden west!"

On witnessing
On doing one thing
When you go home that's an act of revolution

On one small act of social responsibility each day
A practice for all baby boomers and baby boomer babies

Not what you're already doing or do as a matter of habit
But something more and out of habit

Read in the dark!

8 Ongoing

Inching his way down
      Hartford St.
           "a brain and a cane"

"Zen master, cosmic wit, beat original"
"religious Falstaff"
"cranky, wacky, tender, finicky"
"Buddhist abbot, language poet, beat affiliate"
"The most formally radical of the Beat poets"

(Ginsberg warned me about using too many "buzzwords")

        Allen, get out of my poem!
    You're dead and Whalen is still alive

    Still here among us

          June 23, 1999, 11:41

9 Pilgrims

Keep not silence at my tears
For I am a stranger with Thee,
A sojourner, as all my fathers were
Book Of Psalms, XXXIX, l.13

I

I'm going to meet the poet on Hartford St.
Look over his works
Compile them into a book of how many hours
        I don't know, but patience leads
                        I follow. . .

*

"Joy and high finance. The police ran out
gross philosophical denial" <Philip Whalen>

"It glows in the dark
                    like the willow tree hangs
NIRVANA = 'bathing'
Specifically the bathing of elephants" <Ingalls>

                    "The symbol of the state
Elephant fording a river" <Legge>

*

Buddhist abbot cloistered in hospice

Let's drink tea
   watch the barbecue in the garden
       smolder with carcinogens
     I listen to the poet hum Bach
   He despises Schumann and Schubert

Nearly blind with an irascible kindness

*

Don't strain, there's time
   twenty four years of breathing
        to read

   patience, boy, or leave
      We'll work two days a week

*

When you're stoned
  be careful
    of stepping on inspiration

   posting bills, metered parking, speeding
    handguns & condoms

*

A slice of Mexican sugar-coated guava
Manuscript on clumsy card table

Fat man in a T-shirt and loose trousers
Red, purple and blue scrolls hang on walls
Agate found at the beach
                                        polished

Letter from Donald Allen about Kerouac

"Do you mind if I tape this?" I ask
            "Yes, I would *not* be comfortable"

He began recollections with *Three Satires*
Stopped in 1960 where these poems begin
Some published in *The Kindness Of Strangers*
Some in broadsides, little mags, ignored

2

Roshi says,

                altering
                one's breathing manipulates a group

                        *

Enter voice mail jail
                Choose course in labyrint

*

You are my Icarus!
        But never get to fly

      deep sigh, deep breath, eyes closed
      look up at heaven, ohhh
      there you go, just ease out of your body
      ease out of flabby body
      float up above   floating through the garden

      Over purple flowers horning up

And the man who looks like William Burroughs
And the man in black leather and sunglasses

      San Francisco, Chinatown
      Me and Michael McClure
            at tow-yard bailing out my car

         A moment of mutual generosity

               inhaling rain

     *

Toast to the ascending spirit!

*

Melodies, nucleic acids, genetically altered

    Linked beauty
    takes an honored seat

      I hear noises
    They are what I think they are

      I don't need to record them

I'm sitting and writing, it's the same sound

      everyday
    except for the wind & a few

               rain

              drops

*

VISIT #3, ZENSHIN'S GARDEN

      echium, or tower of jewels, *agapanthus*
      roses, bamboo escaping, ginko tree

    Look back at amethyst crystal cluster as we go out

"I shouldn't go without my cane"
                on uneven brick-path to plum harvest

Orange, ripe, sweet, ready, we go out

                Sunny walk to lunch

        Eggplant and ground pork
Long beans and chicken in black bean sauce
                                Steamed rice

                3

"It has nothing to do with poetry, Fuck you!"
McClure says, "Fuck you! You should have told me
it was a big, huge piece of work, massive work!
You just call out of nowhere, want to know what I think!"

                        *

        Save your patience for the head man

                        *

    Lew Welch,

            lost half the time, worrying
        about his mother's furniture, his inheritance

the right, fair play, freezers
on the front and back porch
freezer inside
full of frozen foods, pointless waste

She gave him $150 sports-coat
when he'd rather have the money

deception
wild energy

disappearance in the woods
loaded and mythic

. . .it's the way they saw
the poem, a mythic entity with

powerful associations

Why do they tell me stories about you, Lewie?
Were you the child they wept for when the world burned?

*

So I learn their approach

sit with them, read their syntax
write my own

What's my syntax?

look like, taste like
                smell like, feel like?

        When you don't use your senses
    you just know

                        5/29/93–6/16/93 Pacifica
                        6/23/1999 Boulder

June 28: THE HERO

In Latvia they're melting
statues of Lenin into tiny bells

        and selling them to tourists
        because they don't know

    what else to do with so many

statues of a man
who no longer has meaning

July 3: SCIENTIFIC FACT

asleep
in a chair

in the garden
under a baseball cap

I'm supposed to be
dreaming

August 10: IMPULSES & OBSESSIONS

Be good and you will be rewarded
The dog will follow you around
nudging your hand
with damp affection for a scratch
behind the ear
and your hand will smell
because he hasn't had a bath in 2 weeks

End of thought

I broke a bud vase today
It used to be my father's shot glass
There's sure enough to be bad luck
And I want to clean everything
The stove, every dusty greasy crack

Break the coffee pot

Sympathy is scarce, affection
scarcer, money scarcist but whether
it's broken or out of reach
it isn't enough to screw yourself up
about or go to Japan for Salvation

Bacteria, rod-like
with fancy scientific name
has taken up residency in the body of the monk
In ten days it must be dead and carried out
or mistreatment of the holy bard
will be continued

*

drip   drip

      sucking ginger-ale from articulated straw

drip   drip

sun rises on bed motorized
mocking a foothill the body wraps in and out of linen geology

      until

          drip   drip

scrambled eggs assassinated
and muffins that make one ashamed of being an Englishmen
roll in like death

*

"I lack moral fiber"

      So you put yourself through this?

"Yes, and if I make it very hard on myself
  I hope to become more fibrous"

      So that's why you're building up poundage?
      To test your limits?

He grins maliciously, "Yes"

August 25: WHO KNOWS

You can't teach poetry

        But you can: 1) give a good reading list, show
                     multiple styles

                2) teach writer to distance self
                  from work

                3) knock down blocks
                  you have to keep writing

                *

     East wing hospital seated in chair
        I peel an orange

"When is Penguin going to put you on staff?" he asks
                         after successful event

How did I do it (book dealers want to know)
Fill up the house with book buying poetry lovers?

                *

        I didn't write these poems
        they're not mine
        they belong to Philip Whalen

*

The Butterfly Buddha
   sits on my head

  I'm a pedestal for inspiration
  witness of wise elders and
  coming greats
     making nests

    while I dust branches
     make a place on shelves
  ecstatic
     become a small town
      librarian

August 29: SPILLS

French fries, carrots, chicken and
broadside of P. Glenn Whalen's Dietary Manifesto
in hospital Rm. 520

South window fog rolling down over Twin Peaks
spills into slow evolutionary current
of Literature

11/12
SAT. / SUN.
SEPTEMBER, 1999

Mt. Zion again
1:45 p.m.
He's sleeping
Infection back
They gave him a spinal tap
Fever, irregular heartbeat
Between dreams
He's not sure if I'm here
or if I'm a dream
He likes the feel of my hand
on his head
"I feel frail"

I sit beside him
This is the body of poetry
Intravenous tubed
Cathetered
I.D. bracelet

Shutters on street window rattle
Orange, yellow, red, white striped privacy curtain
Only one body in this room

I threw the burger in the garbage
Ate the shrimp fried rice
My fortune cookie:
"Good health will be yours for a long time"

Searching for an infection
Raise head, cover feet
Lower feet, lower head
Flat roll down to

CATSCAN

"Terrible noise, worse than TV"

Hall calls and bells, phones
Groans
Does anyone understand
he would feel better if
he were not left alone?
Does anyone understand
he's chosen a bachelor's life
in a Land of Zenbos?
All relatives dead?
Except a sister in San Diego
smoking cigarettes in front of TV
as frail as he is

       I brush his full upper dentures
       and partial lowers
       Become increasingly aware
       There's nothing here but a poet

September 15-16: RING CONSPIRACY

I come in and he's all freaked out
from paranoid dreams about Sinn Fein
buzz sawing hospital gonna blow it up
Bad men and a couple of old Irish ladies
tearing the place down until the whole
California Heath System collapses

*

Nearly 2 p.m.
He hasn't eaten since the night before, weakening
They come to get him
Take the turquoise and silver ring from his hand

  "No jewelry, no jewelry, give it to your friend"

He slips it off his finger
I feel the power in the ring as I slip it on
I feel beautiful and safe

"I've got your ring," I remind him
so he doesn't wake up wondering
what happened to his magic
I take the ring home, wash it in anti-bacterial soap
Wrap it in tissue, put it somewhere safe

I call after dinner
We decide it's best we both rest
and meet tomorrow for pork noodles
I'll bring back the ring then

*

I'm at his side wearing the ring
He whispers in my ear to wash my hands
with blue disinfectant at the door
to avoid further contamination

Blood pressure: 139 over 86

They've given up looking
for the source of the hidden meanies
Aim for massive attack

drip, drip

(SNORE)

Up from the street:
"Get off the fucking phone & drive asshole!"

Am I a bodhisattva or a shabbos goy?

"A lap of dead breakfast
and a telephone hidden under the blankets
They're moving me to the skilled nursing wing"

       Well, that's the right direction
       Better than the morgue

"I don't think at the morgue they fuss with you so
much, or so noisy"

       How do you feel?

"The same, tired (at other times `lumpy')
They're keeping me 12 more days"

       At least I'll know where to find you
       when I get back

"I guess"

       *

       SFO airport to LA
       for celebratory reading
       at Beyond Baroque

The Diamond Noodle, p. 64:
u) World of Letters (editing & publishing,
criticism, journalism, all the public and
annoying side of writing)
v) Art World, ie. the mechanical, public side
of it: the gallery, theater, the concert hall & c

*

Mr. Whaaleen? Mr. Whaaleen?
Do you know where you are?

"Rome!"

"How can ya mess up macaroni & cheese?
And they put these big green peas next to it
to make it look scary"

Nancy brought you a burger
yesterday

"I don't remember"

Are you not remembering a lot?

"Yes"

Well, I won't let you forget
anything important

"I'm getting old and my memory is going"

Did you not remember
before you went into the hospital?

"Yes"

*

MOTEL TELEPHONE INTERZONE

What shall I tell people
at the reading tomorrow?

"I've said"

That's what you want me to say?
'I've said'?

"Yes"

September 22: AUTUMN EQUINOX

Day & night length even

Reporting the worst
The worst occurs

They don't want him back at Page St.

Diane di Prima says:
"What do they think Sangha is?
When Suzuki Roshi was here he told them
that in Japan they send their sick
or insane to monasteries in the country to live
But they don't buy it here
Here they dump you on the street"

But nothing is
as simple as it
seems

You go out and get your Buddhism at the mall
Happy & Young & Healthy

& Heartless

This has nothing to do with Buddhism
more to do with the need for an

EXTENDED CARE FACILITY

And though everyone *tries*
success
is impossible
because the system's
got bugs in it
and *oh,*

                                          my aching hip
                           has a kink in it

SIGH

          The sun grays his whiskers
          through the blinds

                The bottom line
                It's about money

September 24: HEART SUTRA

Dharma transmission:
"another maniac unleashed, alas!"

Buddhism in America
"The upper middle way"

    Old Hippie

        say someone gives you roses
and you're allergic to roses
can you still be romantic about roses?

Generosity, Humanity, Heart

    What is the Heart Sutra?

  it's the body being passed overhead
above a crowd
of politicians and power–mad bureaucrats
    by the keepers of the faith

      *

    Oceanly Cosmos
    Buddhist Disco
    What is Sangha?

Ecology of Permission
Poolside, Bedside
All sides inside & out
Dharma, Karma
Parmagian cheese
Oh, Rome,
the hospital is closing
& patients in the extended nursing
wing are listening to the visiting
keyboardist play
"Old Man River"

*

talisman
Heart Sutra
huge mass of Buddhist philosophy
condensed into a few lines
reduced to a mantra:

"Gone, Gone
  Gone beyond
  Gone beyond beyond
  Hail . . ."

September 28: WHEN YOU'RE IN LOVE

Happy to see you home

"There's no home"

That's part of your life

"It's all one life. I wouldn't subscribe to that for very long"

I'm sorry

"There's no reason to apologize when you're in love"

October 9: BOWS

"Goddamn fucking shit turkey!"
I don't get paid to hurry

You got ideas?
Tell me what kind of ideas you got?

"The further you get from the source
of the religion the stranger it gets"

There's nothing to understand
just "Chinese poppycock!"

"Buddhalogical, philosophical concept of karma—
action, every act has consequences
those acts and consequences go on, it doesn't matter
if there's a *person* there or not
There's no *person* no real settled self
And if you *think* that there's a self
then there's nothing but unending entanglements
and confusion. The self is only 5 *skandhas*:
form, feeling, impulses, consciousness, perception
Popular interpretation of karma is
that if you do nice things *now*
you'll be reborn in a Buddhist country
brought up in a pious family and if you decide
to be ordained you're a few steps up
But, pismire, if your acts are bad. While you're living
it pops up and makes you unhappy, effects
the *you* that you *imagine* you are"

"Then there's Parking Karma
like when Lew Welch and Lenore Kandel were together
and Lenore would say, Lew let's go for dinner in Chinatown
and Lew not wanting to go and Lenore saying
come on Lew and Lew complaining about the noise
and crowds and traffic and nowhere to park and Lenore
saying come on Lew and when they finally get there
to Chinatown, Lenore would say her Parking Mantra:

We are nice people
and there is a parking place for us

And boom, over there would be a parking space, and they get a parking space every time and Lew keeps saying Lenore, I don't know how you do that"

There's an explanation for everything

October 18: THERE WAS AN OLD MAN

shoes
buckles and laces
scuff, buff, polish

walking, hiking, climbing

thongs

BONG!

leave them at the door

and when he dies
destroy them

where I've been
sticks like gum to my soul

8 1/2 D
10 E

of different orientation
but equal under the eyes of the law
they say

slippers, opera slippers

with backs
forward, reverse & sideways

click your heels 3 times
and you're home

before you put them on, Tex
check for scorpions

dangling from the power line

barefoot and pregnant

who lived in a shoe?
about that glass slipper?

moccasins, clogs
snow shoes

flippers

October 20-21: OCTOBER 20, 1999

Smoked trout
French bread
Salad
Diet cola & diet ginger ale
Michael McClure
Amy Evans McClure
Leslie Scalapino
Tom Carey
Bill Berkson
Bob Ebert
Nancy Victoria Davis
Long stem roses: "From an Admirer"
       Happy Birthday, Phil

October 20-November 19:
CONVERSATION WITH AN INVENTORY

I

UC-Stanford offer for 20 years of handwritten
 and illustrated notebooks by one of the most
 important poets of the past 40 years

from Goethe's *Conversation With Eckermann*—

> *The Present will have its rights; the thoughts and*
> *feelings which daily press upon the poet will and*
> *should be expressed.*
>
> *But if he daily seizes the present, and always treats*
> *with a freshness of feeling what is offered him, he*
> *always makes sure of something good; and, if he sometimes*
> *does not succeed, has at least lost nothing.*
>
> *And be sure you put to each poem the date at*
> *which you wrote it.*
> *I looked at him inquiringly,*
> *to know why this was so important.*
>
> *'Your poems will thus serve,' he said, 'as a diary of your*
> *progress. I have done it for many years, and can see its use'*

October 20, 1999

PARTIAL INVENTORY OF PHILIP WHALEN'S LIBRARY

JOURNALS

1) Sierras, 1957, Newport, 1958
2) 18:I:61, 10:V:62
3) 21:V:62, 6:I:63
4) 10:I:63, 10:VI:63
5) 18:VI:63, 14:XI:63
6) 15:XI:63, 12:IV:64
7) 21:IV:64, 7:II:66
8) Kyoto, September 1967, California, 1967, December 1967, January 1968–July 1968
9) Expense book Japan 21:VII, 69
10) 9–11:vi:66, 10:III–11:VI–1966
11) September 1968, California
12) I:V:69, 16:V:69
13) 9:X–25:XI: 69
14) 17:v:69,30:v:69
15) 15:VIII–8:X:69
16) 27:XI:69–25:I:70
17) 5:II–4:IV:70
18) 5:IV–17:V:70
19) 3:X–15:XI:70
20) 25:VI–12:VIII:70
21) 17:V–25–VI:70
22) 15:12:70, 14:XII: 70
23) 14:XII:70, 25:III: 71
24) 15:III:71, 8:V:71

25) Kyoto / Bolinas, 8:V:71–21:VII:71
26) Portland / Bolinas, 23:VII:71, 8:X:71
27) Albuquerque, 18X:71–29:X71, San Francisco, 19:VII:72
28) 20:VII:72–10:VII:73
29) 10:VIII:73–19:III:74
30) 19:iii:74–3:XII:74
31) 1:1:75– 3:V:76
32) 2:VI:76–2:III:77
33) March 4, 1977, 13:ix:77
34) 25:ix:77–7:II:78
35) 7:II:78–4:vi:78
36) 12:VI:78–2:12:78
37) 3:XII:78–28:II–79
38) 28:II:79–10:VIII:79
39) 10:VIII:79–17:III:80
40) 17:III:80–18:I:81
41) 18:1:81–18:VIII:81
42) 19:VIII:81–13:V:82
43) 14:V:82–8:XII: 82

*

"I like these things, so I put them down
There's no big plan, nothing to understand"

*

Calls from poet–reviewer
ready to brand name
Philip
as an octopus
because he has so many tentacles
and though we imagine these monstrous deep–sea
creatures to swim quickly and pulverize
with great sucking flesh
It's more likely they float upside down and drift,
prey passively acquired
Living like this until one day
they wash upon a beach
a dead spectacle

*

Couldn't sleep last night
Heard the rain and imagined a leak
in the basement
where Philip's journals and books are stored
Imagine the magnificence wash invisibly away
Stunning and sad
to think we can't hold him forever.

*

Journals essential to understanding work of Philip Whalen.
Handwritten poetical and narrative (unknown in print) journals,
written in calligraphic style taught to him at Reed by Lloyd
Reynolds. Include doodles, coloring and collage. Source books for
his most famous poetical works, in perfect condition, warrant
publication in facsimile. 61 journals cover nearly 30 years.

44) 31: I: 84-14:V:84
45) 15:V:84-17:VIII:84
46) 17:VIII:84-30:III:85
47) 31:III:85-10:IX:85
48) 8:VIII:87-1:XI:87
49) 19:XI:87-20:III:88
50) 15:VI:88-24:VIII:89
51) 20:V:86-24:II:87
52) 5:XI:83-30:I:84
53) 11:IX:85-20:V:86
54) 28:VII:83-5:XI:83
55) 17:III:83-28:VII:83
56) 9:XII:82-17:III:83
57) March 1, 1987- August 7, 1987
58) 17:VIII:81-15:VI-82
59) 16:VI:82-22:IX:82
60) 7:I:84-21:XII:87
61) 22:VI:77-3:I:85

BOOKS

Many first editions and association copies from Rexroth, McClure, Waldman, di Prima, Berrigan, Corman Olson, Kyger, Coolidge, Brautigan, Snyder, Notley, Beltrametti, Lew Welch, Allen Ginsberg, Lamantia, Waldman. Very rare broadsides by Joanne Kyger, Lew Welch and Gary Snyder

eg.: "Take Care of My Ghost, Ghost"
    from the letters of Jack Kerouac and Allen Ginsberg

Manuscript copies of Gary Snyder's "Saigo Foreword" and "True Night"

Personal reading copies, paperbacks from Burroughs to Marvel

Personal copies of his own books:

Donald Allen anthology, *Prologemena to the Study of The Universe, Prologemena to the Study of The Universe* (German trans.*), Memoirs of an Interglacial Age, Highgrade, Monday in the Evening, Hands, Joining: A Calligraphic Anthology, Winning His Way or The Rise of William Johnson*

BROADSIDES

Philip Whalen—"Driving Immediately Past", "Dear Mr. President", "Vision of the Bodhisattvas", "Prose Take", "Hymnus Ad Patrem Siniensis", "Hymnus" (Moe's), "Dorjay Quandary", "For Clark Coolidge", "Organized Crime", "In Takagamine", "Tara", "Window Peak"

Assorted printed by Clifford Burke—"Solstice Night", "Solstice:
    Mostly Empty Space", "Dragon Solstice"
Paul Blackburn—"Salutes Philip Whalen"
Amiri Baraka—"Hard Facts"
Frances Butler and Alistair Johnston—"Continually"
Richard Brautigan—"Five Poems"
Drum Hadley—"Smokey & The Bird Watcher", "Rafael
    Ouijada", "Sierra Madre", "A Cattle Inspector",
    "A Cowboy in Town", "Alvin Taylor & Cowdogs"
Allen Ginsberg—"Kral Majales"
Gregory Corso—"Alchemical Poem"
Joanne Kyger—"The Fool in April", "September", "Oy"
    (personal letter), "The persimmons are falling"
Michael McClure—"Oh Accident", "Winter Solstice", "Berkeley
Song", "The Stitching Letter"
Alice Notley—"Mornings I wonder if I" (art by Schneeman)
Gary Snyder—"Dear Mr. President", "Axe Handles", "Anasazi",
    "Spell Against Demons", "The Lesson We Learn",
    "Smokey Bear Sutra", "Two Logging Songs"
Lew Welch—"Springtime in the Rockies", "Richer than the
    Richest Falconer", "This is Written", "Inflation",
    "I Saw Myself"

*

How Philip apologizes for his mood, feels
he has no right to be cranky
I offer to come back next week, tell him jokes
"At 2 bits a whack?"
Yea, but they're gonna be dollah jokes

More than 2 months in hospital
Home now, carrying intravenous fanny pack
What I call his mythology
"Isn't doing me any good" he says
I give him massage, neck, head, face and back
while Nancy reminds him to breathe

*

Dear ?.?.:
If you're going to give a send up to a bunch of your buddies then I hope you'll add Big Bridge to your list. Not only have I backed you fuckers up but I created a forum for "animated realism" that does not exist elsewhere, with the same magnitude, the same roots and overlapping, online. It may seem odd for you to hear me plug Big Bridge this way, or even make an issue out of it, or maybe it's just me not feeling comfortable about having to blow my own horn, but I realize that if I don't speak up like P. or S. or L. or the others, then I'll be swept aside, dismissed. I'm not as comfortable as you all are beating your chests and inserting yourself in the dialogue. But I'm learning. I hope you hear me and understand that I'm way serious. It's a bit of a joke to be getting hand-jobs left and right and never getting kissed.
So kiss me. MR

*

Philip's journals need to be published

October 30, 1999

*

I joke about selling his dentures for $10,000
"I want my teeth back!" he shouts,
for fear I raise him to the heavens

My muscular wings of condor astral toucan macaw
hummingbird iridescent heron eagle
pounding the ether
lifting him naked, praised without shame:

"Put me down, put me down, it's wrong
for me to be held up so, it means nothing to me,
these things mean nothing to me!"

NO, I won't put you down you sweet bundle of gold
sugar-cubes, hive of sun & divine god-ness!

November 1, 1999

*

sort, organize 500 letters, box them for Bancroft Library

*

A poet, buddhist, yelled at me, apologized
Philip yelled at the poet, pressure mounting

I need to go over there and tell him jokes and reminisce

He's looking at his own quest
"I better join the Neptune Society real quick."

*

Found another journal in a box

    62)   19:X:80–8:VII:89

LETTERS

Several hundred letters from friends and colleagues including:
Gary Snyder, Joanne Kyger, Allen Ginsberg, Michael McClure,
Andrew Schelling, Duncan McNaughton, Alice Notley,
Ron Loewinsohn, Tom Raworth, Bob LaVigne, Bob Kaufman,
Lawrence Ferlinghetti

Included is a very large file of letters from Franco Beltrametti.

Also letters from publishers and printers: Alastair Johnston,
Donald Allen, Michael Sherrick, Brooding Heron, James Koller,
Clifford Burke and Dave Haselwood. Letters from Grey Fox.
Letters from Zephyr. Also many letters from his Aunt may be
important for biography

*

PHOTOGRAPHS

Many family photos (family and baby pictures)
Bolinas and Sourdough Mountain period pictures
Pictures from readings with Lew Welch and Allen Ginsberg
Pictures from Santa Fe
Pictures of him taken by friends

*

FINE PRINT

"Supplication for the Rebirth of the Vidyadhara
Chogyam Trungpa, Rimpoche" by Allen Ginsberg
association copy, boxed scroll, Big Bridge Press.
Man/Women by Joanne Kyger and Michael Rothenberg
association copy, Big Bridge Press
Temple of Flora, Whalen section with artist proof by Jim Dine
from Arion Press

*

ROUGH DRAFT MANUSCRIPTS AND NOTES

Invisible Idylls, Goofbook for Jack Kerouac, "Sandblast"
unpublished manuscripts, attempts, "spitballs" that don't stick

> *Philip says, "Spitballs?"*
> *I say, Yes, that's what you called them*
> *"Don't get attached to that idea"*

Type draft and prose takes of *Scenes of Life at the Capital*
Handwritten Notes and Investigations
Project Proposals
Hype List
Fragments
Handwritten Text to Aram Saroyan Collaboration:
                                    The Children

Various reviews, rights and permissions, Reed Archive notes

*

LITERARY JOURNALS

Many original literary journals where his work was first
published along with well-known poets and writers including,
Kerouac, Ginsberg, Beckett, Berkson, Olson, Rexroth, McClure,
you name it

November 2, 1999

II

E-MAIL AT LEAST TO THE CURRENTLY AWAKE

I ask Philip, "how one faces impermanence with equanimity?"
He says, "watch your breath, sit quietly and practice." National
Park Service wants to raise my rent, put me in a smaller pot.
"The dill plant lives, the airplane/My alarm clock, this ink/
I won't go away." Michael McClure drops by for milk and cook-
ies, raids Philip's medicine cabinet but all he can find are antibiot-
ics. What's happened to the beat generation? Literary
Life in the Golden West needs an addendum. Now kooks and
weirdos can't even stand on their heads for a rush. Another note
from Philip about WCW who comes to Reed College circa
1950. Philip puts a few poems together for critique. One master
instructing the bud to grow, push out daring beyond the known,
and Philip takes it to heart becomes the maddening scent of an
impossible flower, creates his own ecology of permission.

*

ATTACHMENT

Is clinging to life greed?
"It's clinging that's the problem
Attachment is a better word than greed"

Clean electric razor-head
Pork & chicken chow mien
Water purple-veined *phalaenopsis* in sink

Make me a promise, ok?
If you're going to die
wait until I come back from Miami

November 5, 1999

*

BURGER TREK

The man wants to spend the night
with his best friend's girlfriend

> "What's the big deal? Just wash it out
> after you use it. What are ya, narrow-minded?"

Step by step with walker
Crack in pavement, chink in walk
up 18th to Castro St.
Painful arthritis, kink in back
It's further and further
I feel the impossibility
of making it there to Slider's
for burger, onion and mustard

So the doctor cuts into the abscess on his chest

"Smells terrible like rotten hamburger meat"

Ugh!

"Oh, ya got a sensitive stomach?" he smiles

Repeat after me 3X:
    Impermanence with equanimity
    Impermanence with equanimity
    Impermanence with equanimity

        In the face of a crisis in faith
    No afterlife, reincarnation or spirit world

His mother died when he was a boy
Raised by his grandmother and father
They didn't care much for each other
Post-depression era

        Take me back to Jesus!

"These people! The sicker I get the more
    they want from me"

        Send them away!
        Oh, I'm so lonely

Send them away!
Take me back to Jesus!

What would a boy so grand and sensitive have to be ashamed of?
He ate a lot, maybe too much, but caused no one to starve

    "Thanks for lunch, it was splendid"

November 6, 1999

*

SUPER NATURAL CALL

Joanne Kyger calls
We talk about
Christ

November 8, 1999

*

Bancroft Library buys archives

*

    All gone, great memories gone
    "Why am I so lonely? Leave me alone"

Suzi, Philip and I sit for Thai take-out
Green curry chicken, chicken saté

Wait for Norman to join us, he's late
"Roshi Baker and Trungpa Rimpoche

always arrived late, made others wait
cause they had all the marbles and everyone

else was left sucking the hind tit"

November 24- December 1: JACUZZI

Mother comes in my room, bitches about anything
3 weeks in Miami
Too soon to be objective, performance not over
Sit on balcony
Mother comes out, "What are you mad at?'

Thanksgiving weekend:
What's normal family life?

Look up from chlorine pool at *pittisporum* leaves
Natural world in natural state increasingly evasive
Cultivated, paved Florida
Mostly, I'm waiting for the human race to die off
There's a poem in that

Pork & beans:
Philip's choice Thanksgiving meal

HOWARD

Howard wore
7 hats at one
time and looked
good in all of them
But who the hell
is Howard?

December 6, 1999

PORTRAIT

With desire, when wanting
what you can't have

takes your head off

you're too overwhelmed
to have something up your sleeve

SOCIOLOGY

My favorite word in English?
"Lasagna"

December 10, 1999

EMERSON

"Emerson liked to doodle but never knew what to do with it"

December 11, 1999

ISSAN SAID

'Everybody gets what they deserve whether they deserve it
or not'

December 12, 1999

OCEAN RESTAURANT

calm down
remember to breathe
nightmare heebeegeebees
pounding bed shouting
Identity Crisis

Phil on Clement St. :
"Goddamn, I'm sick of these goddamn crippled legs"

at a snail's pace
amidst hubbub holiday shopping
Chinese soy sauce, shrimp chow mien
no time to buy black mushrooms
parked in bus stop
hurry, hurry,
no place to go, hungry, hungry

just keep taking those pills, antibiotics
"Dr. S. embarrassed he can't find the vein"
more blood for the record

what you can't remember
you write down
hurry, hurry, hungry

December 15, 1999

GARDEN PARTY

6 billion people crowd around one TV set
ready to pop the cork
on the Second Millenium
It's very noisy
and few can keep a tune or hold their liquor

It's wrong to hold a grudge, he said,
Check it at the door, acknowledge your sins
But what about extenuating circumstances? I ask,
unable to recall any real crime
"I try to stay busy"

I've confused the issue
from the beginning, brainwashed
It's a Christian conspiracy of clocks and calendars
I'll have no part of that
Dump the TV set, forget what I imagined
Step into the garden. Always a celebration

December 17, 1999

SUSTENANCE

Beef Stew Lo Mien
and Shredded Duck Porridge
with Philip Whalen

December 21, 1999

WHOLE NORTANABLE

2 slices of chocolate ganache, dream fries
So very important

I've lost my taste for romance, appetite for love
Complicated motivations

There's joy in Lact–Aid & Pizza
Savoring a fork of private time

Easy to digest, immaculately prepared
Before I go to sleep, a poem

December 27, 1999

All 1000 lb. Crystal Ball Drop

In Times Square

All "The Future That Wasn't"

All Dystopia and Caviar

All "Sounds Like Sociology"

All "Things To Come", "Just Imagine"

All Y2K Buddha Dharma

All Mystic Jewish Wisdom

All-American Century

All Trippy Affairs and Despairs

All Valium and Legal Pot

All Guns and Zombies

All Astronauts and Movie Stars

All Silence and Song

All Ecology and Liberty

All That In Summary Is Possible

December 31: ALL

Happy New Year!

December 31, 1999— 8:30 p.m.

Celebrations around the planet
TV: 1 million Times Square, 2 million in Rio
Washington Monument, 108 Temple Bells in Tokyo
Brandenburg Gate, Red Square
Circle Dance in Tuscon

Greetings from Internet:
Hawaiian music
Electric pineapple slides skyward
Fireworks, confetti, screams and kisses
Aerial search for lost probe on Mars

Lobster, dungeness crab, caviar, chocolate panache
Paint matrushkas with Nancy, Elya, Cosmos, Mark & David
Stanley (the dog) in millenium glasses
Change barely detectable

January 1, 2000—12:00 p.m.

31·IV·59

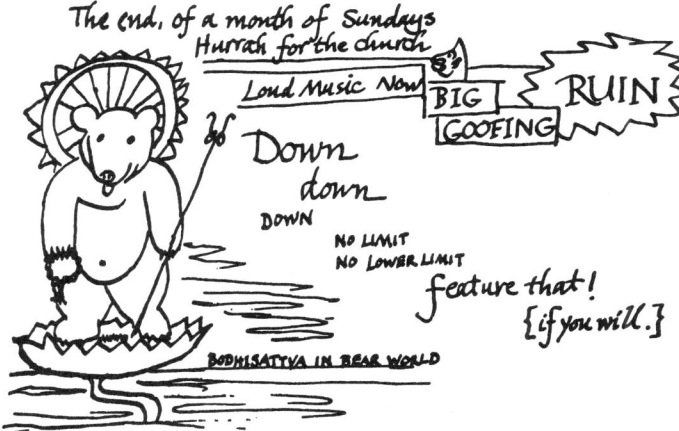

The end of a month of Sundays
Hurrah for the church

Loud Music Now | BIG | RUIN
| GOOFING |

Down
down
DOWN
NO LIMIT
NO LOWER LIMIT
feature that!
{if you will.}

BODHISATTVA IN BEAR WORLD

Philip Whalen

COLOPHON

Set in BEMBO, a face by Monotype
based on the type cut by Francesco Griffo
in 1495 for Aldus Manutius, master printer
of Venice. Stanley Morison named this revival
after Cardinal Bembo, whose book *Der Aetna*
used the orignal roman that this font emulates.
From the Italian Renaissance and its pen nib
stroke to the hot metal type renaissance of the
early 20th century, the letterforms persist in
their clarity and relaxed elegance.

Book design by J. Bryan

Born in Miami Beach, Florida in 1951, Michael Rothenberg is a poet and songwriter. He has been an active environmentalist in the San Francisco Bay Area for the past 25 years, where he cultivates orchids and bromeliads at his nursery, Shelldance. His broadside "Elegy for the Dusky Seaside Sparrow" was selected Broadside of the Year by *Fine Print Magazine*. The broadside of his poem "Angels" was produced in limited edition by Hatch Show Prints as part of The Country Music Foundation's museum resources. His songs have appeared in the films *Shadowhunter*, *Black Day Blue Night* and *Outside Ozona*. He is also editor and co-founder of Big Bridge Press and *Big Bridge*, an online magazine. Michael Rothenberg divides his time between Pacifica, California and Miami, Florida and is on the constant lookout for bottle caps and pennies for his son Cosmos.